A Gift for:

_____

_____

From:

_____

_____

Contents

Foreword

I had to share this treasure chest of promises with you. Many days these words of comfort provided the assurance that God cares for me so much that He designed a plan to meet all of my needs. His special provisions for you and I are often referred to as "promises."

Some promises become activated the moment we accept Jesus Christ as our personal Lord and Savior, while others lie dormant waiting to be activated by a principle that we put into action.

You may ask "How do I activate these benefits in my life?" Friend, the wonderful thing about God is that He does not hide treasure maps wrapped up in mystery and intrigue, or lead us on a wild scavenger hunt. But unfortunately, many people never experience the joy of God's promises because of their ignorance of God's Word. The Scriptures declare, "My people perish because of a lack of knowledge." This does not have to be the case! God gives us ready access to these treasures in a clear manuscript that we call the Bible. And even when we get in trouble or go through hardships and struggles, we don't have to go into a trial and failure mode; we can activate the promises of God by invoking the principles that release the promises. This book will show you how.

The value of knowing God's promises is that we have an assurance that God watches over His Word to perform it. He doesn't "forget" His promises. His promises leap into action when principles are activated. Conversely, when principles are violated, the promises lie dormant.

Many promises have an "if-then" clause. For example:

"**If** My people who are called by My name will humble themselves, and pray and seek My face, and turn from their wicked ways, then I will hear from heaven, and will forgive their sin and heal their land" (2 Chron. 7:14).

The principle or "if": Humble ourselves, pray, seek God's face, and turn from wickedness.

The promise or "then": God will forgive our sins and heal our land.

Use this Book of Promises to help you activate principles that will release your promises.

In your desire to live the abundant life, *I Promise You* will take you from the sidelines of watching other people get blessed and position you as an eligible participant to enjoy God's promises.

Put God's Word to the test. He honors His Word above His name, and He will watch over His Word to perform it. Be blessed as you come into a fuller knowledge and deeper understanding of God's provisions for you.

Love,

Connecting to the Promises through Your Covenant

Did you know that the plan of salvation places you in covenant with our Heavenly Father? Through your adoption into the Kingdom of God you have been given a divine inheritance. Did you know that God desires for you to prosper and be in good health even as your soul prospers? He does! Take some time to become familiar with all of your privileges that are outlined in various covenants throughout the Word of God.

What exactly is a covenant, you may ask? A covenant is a legally binding agreement between two or more parties to solidify a commitment. In order for a covenant to be valid, all parties must not only agree to it, but they must also perform their individual duties as outlined in the covenant.

God's Word is full of covenants for our lives, each relating to a promise that God will perform under certain conditions such as our obedience, repentance, faith, and so on.

We activate promises by initiating principles. Here is a simple principle that most of us are familiar with. *We give to receive.* This principle is outlined in the promise 'Give and it shall be given unto you". As simple as this may seem, God is bound by this covenant to fulfill the promises of His Word.

God is not a man, that He should lie, Nor a son of man, that He should repent. Has He said, and will He not do? Or has He spoken, and will He not make it good?

PROVERBS 23:19

A covenant requires commitment. God is committed to His Word. The Bible says He has fidelity to it – He is married to it. Though a breach of contract may occur on the part of people, God eagerly watches over His Word waiting to perform that which He has promised. Because of our imperfect nature we often "plead the promises while we violate the principles" expecting to get the desired results. Not so! Despite God's infinite mercy we are still held to our part of the agreement.

Purpose in your heart today to uphold your part of the contract. Live a life that is holy and pleasing to God, then experience His blessings.

"Now to Him who is able to do exceedingly abundantly above all that you can ask or think, according to His power that works in us"!

EPHESIANS 3:20

*Today is the day
to rise up and claim the
promises of God.*

Abuse

*A wound is an event, but healing
is a process. Don't bypass the process
for the progress. The journey is important.*

If anyone is in Christ, he is a new creation; old things have passed away; behold, all things have become new.

2 CORINTHIANS 5:17

I will be a Father to you, And you shall be My sons and daughters.

2 CORINTHIANS 6:18

He delivers me from my enemies.
You also lift me up above those who rise against me;
You have delivered me from the violent man.
Therefore I will give thanks to You, O LORD.

PSALM 18:48-49

You are my hiding place;
You shall preserve me from trouble;
You shall surround me with songs of deliverance.

PSALM 32:7

_____

*I have two words for you to use when the
enemy brings your past to your
remembrance: So what?*

_____

Let the wicked forsake his way,
And the unrighteous man his thoughts;
Let him return to the LORD,
And He will have mercy on him;
And to our God,
For He will abundantly pardon.

ISAIAH 55:7

Before I formed you in the womb I knew you;
before you were born I sanctified you.

JEREMIAH 1:5

Addictions

*You have been given the power to say
"no" to sin and "yes" to God.*

Our old man was crucified with Him, that the
body of sin might be done away with, that we
should no longer be slaves of sin. For he who
has died has been freed from sin.

ROMANS 6:6-7

He who has begun a good work in you will
complete it until the day of Jesus Christ.

PHILIPPIANS 1:6

If the Son makes you free, you shall be free indeed.

JOHN 8:36

When we accept Christ, we don't immediately die to all sinful impulses and desires. We must die to the flesh daily.

Put off, concerning your former conduct, the old man which grows corrupt according to the deceitful lusts, and be renewed in the spirit of your mind, and . . . put on the new man which was created according to God, in true righteousness and holiness.

EPHESIANS 4:22-24

For which cause we faint not; but though our outward man perish, yet the inward man is renewed day by day.

2 CORINTHIANS 4:16

Adversity

---

*God can use a negative to bring
about a positive. He can reverse the adverse.*

He only is my rock and my salvation;
He is my defense;
I shall not be greatly moved.

Psalm 62:2

In all these things we are more than conquerors
through Him who loved us. For I am persuaded
that neither death nor life, nor angels nor
principalities nor powers, nor things present nor
things to come, nor height nor depth, nor any
other created thing, shall be able to separate us
from the love of God.

Romans 8:37-39

Whatever is born of God overcomes the world.
And this is the victory that has overcome the
world-our faith.

I JOHN 5:4

Your set-back is a set-up for your come back.

Beloved, do not think it strange concerning the
fiery trial which is to try you, as though some
strange thing happened to you; but rejoice to
the extent that you partake of Christ's
sufferings, that when His glory is revealed, you
may also be glad with exceeding joy.

I PETER 4:12-13

But He knows the way that I take;
When He has tested me, I shall come forth as gold.

JOB 23:10

The righteous cry out, and the LORD hears,
And delivers them out of all their troubles.

PSALM 34:17

If God promises you peace, don't settle for anxiety, worry, and stress.

When you pass through the waters, I will be
   with you;
And through the rivers, they shall not
   overflow you.
When you walk through the fire, you shall not
   be burned,
Nor shall the flame scorch you.
For I am the LORD your God.

ISAIAH 43:2

Affiliations/Friends

Show me your friends and I'll tell you who you are.

The righteous should choose his friends carefully, for the way of the wicked leads them astray.

PROVERBS 12:26

Do not be conformed to this world, but be transformed by the renewing of your mind, that you may prove what is that good and acceptable and perfect will of God.

ROMANS 12:2

Have no fellowship with the unfruitful works of darkness, but rather expose them.

EPHESIANS 5:11

Let us cast off the works of darkness, and let us put on the armor of light. Let us walk properly, as in the day, not in revelry and drunkenness, not in lewdness and lust, not in strife and envy.

ROMANS 13:12-13

The fear of the LORD is the beginning of wisdom, and the knowledge of the Holy One is understanding.

PROVERBS 9:10

He who walks with wise men will be wise, but the companion of fools will be destroyed.

PROVERBS 13:20

A true friend sees beyond what you are to what you can be.

Greater love has no one than this, than to lay down one's life for his friends. These things I command you, that you love one another.

JOHN 15:17

A man who has friends must himself be friendly, but there is a friend who sticks closer than a brother.

PROVERBS 18:24

Do you not know that friendship with the world is enmity with God? Whoever therefore wants to be a friend of the world makes himself an enemy of God.

JAMES 4:4

Bear one another's burdens, and so fulfill the law of Christ.

GALATIANS 6:2

Friends create comfort.
Enemies create challenges.

Anger

Let all bitterness, wrath, anger, clamor, and evil speaking be put away from you, with all malice. And be kind to one another, tenderhearted, forgiving one another, even as God in Christ forgave you.

EPHESIANS 4:31-32

The discretion of a man makes him slow to anger, and his glory is to overlook a transgression.

PROVERBS 19:11

"Be angry, and do not sin": do not let the sun go down on your wrath.

EPHESIANS 4:26

He who is slow to wrath has great understanding, but he who is impulsive exalts folly.

PROVERBS 14:29

You can disagree, agreeably.

Now you yourselves are to put off all these:
anger, wrath, malice, blasphemy, filthy language
out of your mouth. COLOSSIANS 3:8

Cease from anger, and forsake wrath;
do not fret—it only causes harm. PSALM 37:8

Do not hasten in your spirit to be angry,
for anger rests in the bosom of fools.

ECCLESIASTES 7:9

Beloved, do not avenge yourselves, but rather
give place to wrath; for it is written, "Vengeance
is Mine, I will repay," says the Lord.

ROMANS 12:19

Bitterness will make you resent other
people's happiness.

Anointing

The anointing is to a child of God
what a phone booth is to Clarke Kent.

He who establishes us with you in Christ and
has anointed us is God, who also has sealed us
and given us the Spirit in our hearts as
a guarantee.

1 CORINTHIANS 1:21-22

The Spirit of the Lord GOD is upon Me,
Because the LORD has anointed Me
To preach good tidings to the poor;
He has sent Me to heal the brokenhearted,
To proclaim liberty to the captives,
And the opening of the prison to those who
are bound.

ISAIAH 61:1

Now I know that the LORD saves His anointed;
He will answer him from His holy heaven
with the saving strength of His right hand.

PSALM 20:6

Your life is preaching a sermon.

But the anointing which you have received from
Him abides in you, and you do not need that
anyone teach you; but as the same anointing
teaches you concerning all things, and is true,
and is not a lie, and just as it has taught you,
you will abide in Him.

I JOHN 2:27

He is the tower of salvation to His king, and
shows mercy to His anointed.

2 SAMUEL 22:51

You have an anointing from the Holy One, and
you know all things.

I JOHN 2:20

When they came, . . . he looked at Eliab and said, "Surely the LORD's anointed is before Him!" But the LORD said to Samuel, "Do not look at his appearance or at his physical stature, because I have refused him. For the LORD does not see as man sees; for man looks at the outward appearance, but the LORD looks at the heart."

1 SAMUEL 16:6-7

You must hear God's voice
until it becomes louder
than any other voice in your life.

Attitude

Your attitude determines your altitude.

Let your conduct be without covetousness;
be content with such things as you have. For He
Himself has said, "I will never leave you nor forsake
you." So we may boldly say: "The LORD is my
helper; I will not fear. What can man do to me?"

To be carnally minded is death, but to be
spiritually minded is life and peace.

ROMANS 8:6

You have turned for me my mourning into
    dancing;
You have put off my sackcloth and clothed me
    with gladness,

Paula White ☙ 31

To the end that my glory may sing praise to You
    and not be silent.
O Lord my God, I will give thanks to
    You forever.

PSALM 30:12-13

Let us not grow weary while doing good, for in
due season we shall reap if we do not lose heart.

GALATIANS 6:9

———————————

*Healing attitudes
set you free to receive wholeness.*

———————————

Cast your burden on the Lord, and He shall
sustain you; He shall never permit the righteous
to be moved.

PSALM 55:22

God is not the author of confusion but of
peace, as in all the churches of the saints.

I CORINTHIANS 14:33

Balance

God is calling us to audit our lives . . .
our lives must be managed.

Come to Me, all you who labor and are heavy
laden, and I will give you rest.
Matthew 11:28

The ways of a man are before the eyes of
the Lord, and He ponders all his paths.
Proverbs 5:21

Restore to me the joy of Your salvation,
And uphold me by Your generous Spirit.
Psalm 51:12

---

*Set realistic expectations for yourself.
Know what you can do
and know how much you can do.*

A man's heart plans his way,
But the LORD directs his steps.

PROVERBS 16:9

"If anyone thirsts, let him come to Me and
drink. He who believes in Me, as the Scripture
has said, out of his heart will flow rivers of
living water."

JOHN 7:37

The wisdom of the prudent is to understand
his way.

PROVERBS 14:8

Bitterness

---

*Ask God for grace
to let go of the bitterness and pain
that others have caused you.*

Looking carefully lest anyone fall short of the grace of God; lest any root of bitterness springing up cause trouble, and by this many become defiled.

HEBREWS 12:15

Repent therefore . . . and pray God if perhaps the thought of your heart may be forgiven you. For I see that you are poisoned by bitterness.

ACTS 8:22-23

And in all these things is the life of my spirit; so You will restore me and make me live. . . . I had great bitterness; but You have lovingly delivered my soul from the pit of corruption.

ISAIAH 38:16-17

*Allow God's love
to pierce through your pain!*

May the God of patience and comfort grant you to be like-minded toward one another, according to Christ Jesus, that you may with one mind and one mouth glorify the God and Father of our Lord Jesus Christ.

ROMANS 15:5

If you have bitter envy and self-seeking in your hearts, do not boast and lie against the truth. This wisdom does not descend from above.

JAMES 3:14-15

Career

You are engineered by God to be a success.

"I am the LORD your God,
Who teaches you to profit,
Who leads you by the way you should go."

ISAIAH 48:17

Trust in the LORD with all your heart,
And lean not on your own understanding;
In all your ways acknowledge Him,
And He shall direct your paths.

PROVERBS 3:5-6

He who tills his land will be satisfied with bread,
but he who follows frivolity is devoid of
understanding.

PROVERBS 12:11

God has a prepared place for prepared people. The difficulty is not preparing the place, but preparing the people.

Commit your works to the Lord, and your thoughts will be established.

PROVERBS 16:3

Through wisdom a house is built,
And by understanding it is established;
By knowledge the rooms are filled
With all precious and pleasant riches.

PROVERBS 24:3-4

You shall remember the Lord your God, for it is He who gives you power to get wealth, that He may establish His covenant which He swore to your fathers, as it is this day.

DEUTERONOMY 8:18

Change

God loves you too much
to leave you the same.

Therefore, if anyone is in Christ, he is a new creation; old things have passed away; behold, all things have become new.

2 CORINTHIANS 5:17

Put off . . . the old man which grows corrupt according to the deceitful lusts, and be renewed in the spirit of your mind, and that you put on the new man which was created according to God, in true righteousness and holiness.

EPHESIANS 4:22-24

Brethren, I do not count myself to have apprehended; but one thing I do, forgetting those things which are behind and reaching forward to those things which are ahead, I press toward the goal for the prize of the upward call of God in Christ Jesus.

PHILIPPIANS 3:13-14

The work of righteousness will be peace, and the effect of righteousness, quietness and assurance forever.

ISAIAH 32:17

Anytime there is change—
there is opportunity.

Do not remember the former things,
Nor consider the things of old.
Behold, I will do a new thing,
Now it shall spring forth;
Shall you not know it?

I will even make a road in the wilderness
And rivers in the desert.

ISAIAH 43:18-19

For sin shall not have dominion over you,
for you are not under law but under grace.
What then? Shall we sin because we are not
under law but under grace? Certainly not!
Do you not know that to whom you present
yourselves slaves to obey, you are that one's
slaves whom you obey, whether of sin leading to
death, or of obedience leading to righteousness?

ROMANS 6:14-16

*You must be willing to disconnect from
your past and move toward the presence of
greatness in your future.*

Character

*Your character is who you are
when no one is looking.*

That you may walk worthy of the Lord, fully
pleasing Him, being fruitful in every good work
and increasing in the knowledge of God.

COLOSSIANS 1:10

But as He who called you is holy, you also be
holy in all your conduct.

1 PETER 1:15

I keep Your precepts and Your testimonies,
for all my ways are before You.

PSALM 119:168

The righteous man walks in his integrity; his children are blessed after him.

PROVERBS 20:7

Create in me a clean heart, O God, and renew a steadfast spirit within me.

PSALM 51:10

When a person lives in the presence of the Lord, he has fixed principles that rule his heart and guide his life.

If we live in the Spirit, let us also walk in the Spirit.

GALATIANS 5:25

You shall be holy, for I the LORD your God am holy.

LEVITICUS 19:2

Therefore, to him who knows to do good and does not do it, to him it is sin.

JAMES 4:17

But we all, . . . are being transformed into the same image from glory to glory, just as by the Spirit of the Lord.

2 CORINTHIANS 3:18

*Who you are
speaks louder than what you have.*

Comfort

Be bold, be strong,
for the Lord your God is with you.

Yea, though I walk through the valley of the
shadow of death, I will fear no evil; for You are
with me; Your rod and Your staff, they comfort me.

PSALM 23:4

Let not your heart be troubled; you believe in
God, believe also in Me.

JOHN 14:1

He heals the brokenhearted and binds up
their wounds.

PSALM 147:3

Blessed be the God and Father of our Lord Jesus
Christ, the Father of mercies and God of all

comfort, who comforts us in all our tribulation, that we may be able to comfort those who are in any trouble, with the comfort with which we ourselves are comforted by God.

2 CORINTHIANS 1:3-4

There's a time to pour out your heart before the Lord and state your case. There's also a time to get up, wipe your tears, and walk away with trust.

Blessed are those who mourn, for they shall be comforted.

MATTHEW 5:4

As one whom his mother comforts, so I will comfort you.

ISAIAH 61:13

You are my hiding place;
You shall preserve me from trouble;
You shall surround me with songs of deliverance.

Oh, how great is Your goodness,
which You have laid up for those who fear You,
which You have prepared for those who trust
  in You.

For I will turn their mourning to joy,
Will comfort them,
And make them rejoice rather than sorrow.

Communication

*You frame your world
by the words you speak.*

Let no corrupt word proceed out of your mouth,
but what is good for necessary edification, that it
may impart grace to the hearers.

EPHESIANS 4:29

Pleasant words are like a honeycomb,
sweetness to the soul and health to the bones.

PROVERBS 16:24

A good man out of the good treasure of his heart
brings forth good; and an evil man out of the evil
treasure of his heart brings forth evil. For out of
the abundance of the heart his mouth speaks.

LUKE 6:45

Whoever guards his mouth and tongue,
keeps his soul from troubles.

PROVERBS 21:23

The truthful lip shall be established forever,
but a lying tongue is but for a moment.

PROVERBS 12:19

A soft answer turns away wrath,
But a harsh word stirs up anger.
The tongue of the wise uses knowledge rightly.

PROVERBS 15:1-2

Let the words of my mouth
and the meditation of my heart
be acceptable in Your sight,
O LORD, my strength and my Redeemer.

PSALM 19:14

———————

Silence cannot be misquoted.

———————

Your heart is a filter
that pollutes or purifies your words.

But I say to you that for every idle word men
may speak, they will give account of it in the
day of judgment.

MATTHEW 12:36

Avoid foolish disputes, genealogies, contentions,
and strivings about the law; for they are
unprofitable and useless.

TITUS 3:9

As long as my breath is in me,
And the breath of God in my nostrils,
My lips will not speak wickedness,
Nor my tongue utter deceit.

JOB 27:3-4

He who would love life and see good days, let
him refrain his tongue from evil, and his lips
from speaking deceit.

1 PETER 3:10

Confessing God's Word

God's Word gives birth to your destiny.

So shall My Word be that goes forth from My mouth; it shall not return to Me void, but it shall accomplish what I please, and it shall prosper in the thing for which I sent it.

ISAIAH 55:11

Let us hold fast the confession of our hope without wavering, for He who promised is faithful.

HEBREWS 10:23

Seeing then that we have a great High Priest who has passed through the heavens, Jesus the Son of God, let us hold fast our confession.

HEBREWS 4:14

The Word of God is living and powerful, and
sharper than any two-edged sword, piercing
even to the division of soul and spirit, and of
joints and marrow, and is a discerner of the
thoughts and intents of the heart.

HEBREWS 4:12

*Your faith will not
rise above your confession.*

These things we also speak, not in words which
man's wisdom teaches but which the Holy
Spirit teaches.

1 CORINTHIANS 2:13

*Stop living by what you feel,
and live by what God says.*

By the Word of the Lord the heavens were made, and all the host of them by the breath of His mouth.

PSALM 33:6

It is the Spirit who gives life; the flesh profits nothing. The words that I speak to you are spirit, and they are life.

JOHN 6:63

For assuredly, I say to you, whoever says to this mountain, "Be removed and be cast into the sea," and does not doubt in his heart, but believes that those things he says will be done, he will have whatever he says.

MARK 11:23

Courage

For every blessing there is testing —
for every opportunity there is adversity.

Wait on the LORD;
Be of good courage,
And He shall strengthen your heart;
Wait, I say, on the LORD!

PSALM 27:14

Most assuredly, I say to you, he who believes in
Me, the works that I do he will do also; and
greater works than these he will do, because I go
to My Father.

JOHN 14:12

Watch, stand fast in the faith, be brave, be
strong. Let all that you do be done with love.

1 CORINTHIANS 16:13

The LORD is good, a stronghold in the day of trouble; and He knows those who trust in Him.

NAHUM 1:7

The LORD will be your confidence,
and will keep your foot from being caught.

PROVERBS 3:26

Be of good courage,
and He shall strengthen your heart,
all you who hope in the LORD.

PSALM 31:24

The Lord is faithful, who will establish you and guard you from the evil one.

2 THESSALONIANS 3:3

In the fear of the LORD there is strong confidence,
and His children will have a place of refuge.

PROVERBS 14:26

———

*The challenges handed to you in life
are trying to push you into your destiny.*

———

Depression

Things might go wrong,
but you don't have to go with them.

The righteous cry out, and the LORD hears,
and delivers them out of all their troubles.

PSALM 34:17

He heals the brokenhearted and binds up
their wounds.

PSALM 147:3

Cast your burden on the LORD, and He shall
sustain you; He shall never permit the righteous
to be moved.

PSALM 55:22

In the world you will have tribulation; but be of
good cheer, I have overcome the world.

JOHN 16:33

---

*When you become so broken you
don't know where to turn, . . . turn to God.*

Weeping may endure for a night,
but joy comes in the morning.

Psalm 30:5

We also glory in tribulations, knowing that
tribulation produces perseverance; and
perseverance, character; and character, hope.
Now hope does not disappoint, because the love
of God has been poured out in our hearts by
the Holy Spirit who was given to us.

Romans 5:3-5

The Lord has comforted His people, and will
have mercy on His afflicted.

Isaiah 49:13

Destiny

You have been liberated from your past
and delivered into your destiny.

I know the thoughts that I think toward you,
says the LORD, thoughts of peace and not of
evil, to give you a future and a hope.

JEREMIAH 29:11

If the Son makes you free, you shall be free indeed.

JOHN 8:36

I can do all things through Christ who
strengthens me.

PHILIPPIANS 4:13

In Him dwells all the fullness of the Godhead
bodily; and you are complete in Him, who is
the head of all principality and power.

COLOSSIANS 2:9-10

There is a deposit of wealth within you waiting to be developed.

I will dwell in them and walk among them. I will be their God, and they shall be My people.

2 CORINTHIANS 6:16

So I will strengthen them in the LORD, and they shall walk up and down in His name.

ZECHARIAH 10:12

Eye has not seen, nor ear heard, nor have entered into the heart of man the things which God has prepared for those who love Him.

1 CORINTHIANS 2:9

Choice, not chance, determines destiny.

Direction

*To hold on to your dream
and fulfill God's plan for your life,
you must keep moving forward.*

If any of you lacks wisdom, let him ask of God,
who gives to all liberally and without reproach,
and it will be given to him.

JAMES 1:5

I will instruct you and teach you in the way you
should go; I will guide you with My eye.

PSALM 32:8

The steps of a good man are ordered by the
LORD, and He delights in his way.

PSALM 37:23

When God speaks to you,
He does so from where you are going—
not from where you are.

For this is God, our God forever and ever;
He will be our guide even to death.

PSALM 48:14

The LORD will guide you continually,
And satisfy your soul in drought,
And strengthen your bones;
You shall be like a watered garden,
And like a spring of water, whose waters do
   not fail.

ISAIAH 58:11

When He, the Spirit of truth, has come, He will
guide you into all truth; for He will not speak
on His own authority, but whatever He hears He
will speak; and He will tell you things to come.

JOHN 16:13

Discipline

---

*To be disciplined means
to do the right thing when you feel like
doing the wrong thing.*

Let a man so consider us as servants of Christ and stewards of the mysteries of God. Moreover it is required in stewards that one be found faithful.

1 CORINTHIANS 4:1-2

Well done, good and faithful servant; you were faithful over a few things, I will make you ruler over many things.

MATTHEW 25:21

Present your bodies a living sacrifice, holy, acceptable to God, which is your reasonable service.

ROMANS 12:1

Be steadfast, immovable, always abounding in the work of the Lord.

1 CORINTHIANS 15:58

The pain of discipline weighs much less than the load of regret.

Great peace have those who love Your law, and nothing causes them to stumble.

PSALM 119:165

Therefore gird up the loins of your mind, be sober, and rest your hope fully upon the grace that is to be brought to you at the revelation of Jesus Christ; as obedient children, not conforming yourselves to the former lusts.

1 PETER 1:13-14

Discouragement

God will renew your life
by renewing your mind.

In this you greatly rejoice, though now for a little
while, if need be, you have been grieved by
various trials, that the genuineness of your faith,
being much more precious than gold that
perishes, though it is tested by fire, may be found
to praise, honor, and glory at the revelation of
Jesus Christ, whom having not seen you love.

1 PETER 1:6-7

You are my hiding place and my shield;
I hope in Your word.

PSALM 119:114

God is my strength and power, and He makes my way perfect.

2 SAMUEL 22:33

That I may know Him and the power of His resurrection, and the fellowship of His sufferings, being conformed to His death.

PHILIPPIANS 3:10

Today is the day to regain your focus. Put your eyes on the future God has for you.

In the day when I cried out, You answered me, and made me bold with strength in my soul.

PSALM 138:3

We do not lose heart. Even though our outward man is perishing, yet the inward man is being renewed day by day. For our light affliction, which is but for a moment, is working for us a far more exceeding and eternal weight of glory.

2 CORINTHIANS 4:16-17

Why are you cast down, O my soul?
And why are you disquieted within me?
Hope in God; for I shall yet praise Him,
the help of my countenance and my God.

PSALM 43:5

———————

*God often breeds greatness
out of the worst situations you can imagine.*

———————

Dreams for Your Life

Stop looking back.
God is pulling you to what's ahead!

Every good gift and every perfect gift is from above, and comes down from the Father of lights, with whom there is no variation or shadow of turning.

JAMES 1:17

Let us hold fast the confession of our hope without wavering, for He who promised is faithful.

HEBREWS 10:23

Seek first the kingdom of God and His righteousness, and all these things shall be added to you.

MATTHEW 6:33

*That same God who gave you your dream
will complete what He has started in you.*

It is God who arms me with strength,
and makes my way perfect.

PSALM 18:32

"For My thoughts are not your thoughts,
Nor are your ways My ways," says the LORD.
"For as the heavens are higher than the earth,
So are My ways higher than your ways,
And My thoughts than your thoughts."

ISAIAH 55:8-9

Now faith is the substance of things hoped for,
the evidence of things not seen.

HEBREWS 11:1

*History makers and world changers
are mere men and women
who followed their dreams.*

*Live your life in pursuit
of the dream God
put inside of you—
a dream only
you can pursue and
only you can fulfill.*

Emotions

There's tremendous freedom
from emotional turmoil when you focus
all your heart, mind, and soul
on praising the Lord.

May the God of all grace, who called us to His
eternal glory by Christ Jesus, after you have
suffered a while, perfect, establish, strengthen,
and settle you.

I PETER 5:10

For we do not have a High Priest who cannot
sympathize with our weaknesses, but was in all
points tempted as we are, yet without sin. Let us
therefore come boldly to the throne of grace,
that we may obtain mercy and find grace to
help in time of need.

HEBREWS 4:15-16

You, Lord, have made me glad through Your work;
I will triumph in the works of Your hands.

PSALM 92:4

God's thoughts toward us are for peace.

I have learned in whatever state I am, to be
content: I know how to be abased, and I know
how to abound. Everywhere and in all things I
have learned both to be full and to be hungry,
both to abound and to suffer need. I can do all
things through Christ who strengthens me.

PHILIPPIANS 4:11-13

Create in me a clean heart, O God,
and renew a steadfast spirit within me.
Do not cast me away from Your presence,
and do not take Your Holy Spirit from me.
Restore to me the joy of Your salvation,
and uphold me by Your generous Spirit.

PSALM 51:10-12

God can use a crisis and a time
of confusion in our lives to bring us
to a decision that will result in a blessing.

The LORD is near to those who have a broken heart,
and saves such as have a contrite spirit.

PSALM 34:18

Light is sown for the righteous,
and gladness for the upright in heart.
Rejoice in the LORD, you righteous,
and give thanks at the remembrance of His
holy name.

PSALM 97:11-12

Failure

---

*Failure is not falling down —
but staying down!*

If I say, "My foot slips," Your mercy, O LORD,
will hold me up.

PSALM 94:18

Deliver me out of the mire,
And let me not sink;
Let me be delivered from those who hate me,
And out of the deep waters.
Let not the floodwater overflow me,
Nor let the deep swallow me up.

PSALM 69:14-15

There is therefore now no condemnation to those
who are in Christ Jesus, who do not walk
according to the flesh, but according to the Spirit.

ROMANS 8:1

By one offering He has perfected forever those who are being sanctified.

HEBREWS 10:14

*Don't confuse your mistakes
with your value as a person.*

In all things we commend ourselves as ministers of God: in much patience, in tribulations, in needs, in distresses.

2 CORINTHIANS 6:4

Surely goodness and mercy shall follow me all the days of my life; and I will dwell in the house of the LORD forever.

PSALM 23:6

*You might be disappointed
if you fail, but you are doomed
if you never try.*

Faith

If you can see the invisible,
you can do the impossible.

By grace you have been saved through faith, and
that not of yourselves; it is the gift of God, not
of works, lest anyone should boast.

EPHESIANS 2:8-9

He did not waver at the promise of God through
unbelief, but was strengthened in faith, giving
glory to God, and being fully convinced that what
He had promised He was also able to perform.

ROMANS 4:20, 21

Now faith is the substance of things hoped for,
the evidence of things not seen.

HEBREWS 11:1

Faith takes you
from promise to performance.

So then faith comes by hearing, and hearing by the Word of God.

ROMANS 10:17

Without faith it is impossible to please Him, for he who comes to God must believe that He is, and that He is a rewarder of those who diligently seek Him.

HEBREWS 11:6

Jesus said to him, "If you can believe, all things are possible to him who believes."

MARK 9:23

It is better to move in faith
than to sit in doubt.

We walk by faith, not by sight.

2 CORINTHIANS 5:7

Faith is developed
by the Word that is deposited.

That the genuineness of your faith, being much more precious than gold that perishes, though it is tested by fire, may be found to praise, honor, and glory at the revelation of Jesus Christ, whom having not seen you love. Though now you do not see Him, yet believing, you rejoice with joy inexpressible and full of glory, receiving the end of your faith-the salvation of your souls.

I PETER 1:7-9

Whatever is born of God overcomes the world. And this is the victory that has overcome the world—our faith.

I JOHN 5:4

Family

We all desire to be listened to . . .
to be hugged . . . to be called
a person of worth . . . to "belong."

Believe on the Lord Jesus Christ, and you will be saved, you and your household.

ACTS 16:31

And if it seems evil to you to serve the LORD, choose for yourselves this day whom you will serve, whether the gods which your fathers served that were on the other side of the River, or the gods of the Amorites, in whose land you dwell. But as for me and my house, we will serve the LORD.

JOSHUA 24:15

Train up a child in the way he should go, and
when he is old he will not depart from it.

PROVERBS 22:6

You, fathers, do not provoke your children to
wrath, but bring them up in the training and
admonition of the Lord.

EPHESIANS 6:4

Make memories with those you love.

Blessed is every one who fears the LORD,
Who walks in His ways.
When you eat the labor of your hands,
You shall be happy, and it shall be well with you.
Your wife shall be like a fruitful vine
In the very heart of your house,
Your children like olive plants
All around your table.
Behold, thus shall the man be blessed
Who fears the LORD.

PSALM 128:1-4

The father of the righteous will greatly rejoice, and
he who begets a wise child will delight in him.

PROVERBS 23:24

These words which I command you today shall
be in your heart. You shall teach them diligently
to your children, and shall talk of them when
you sit in your house, when you walk by the
way, when you lie down, and when you rise up.

DEUTERONOMY 6:6-7

Correct your son, and he will give you rest;
yes, he will give delight to your soul.

PROVERBS 29:17

My son, keep your father's command,
and do not forsake the law of your mother.
Bind them continually upon your heart
tie them around your neck.

PROVERBS 6:20

*You cannot hold others to a standard
you are not willing to live by yourself.*

Fear

Fear has torment while faith has rest.

There is no fear in love; but perfect love casts
out fear, because fear involves torment. But he
who fears has not been made perfect in love.

I JOHN 4:18

Be strong and of good courage; do not fear nor
be dismayed.

I CHRONICLES 22:13

So we may boldly say: "The LORD is my helper;
I will not fear. What can man do to me?"

HEBREWS 13:6

Yea, though I walk through the valley of the
    shadow of death,
I will fear no evil;
For You are with me;
Your rod and Your staff, they comfort me.

PSALM 23:4

---

*Fear, worry, and anxiety
are interest paid in advance for something
you will probably never own!*

God has not given us a spirit of fear, but of
power and of love and of a sound mind.

2 TIMOTHY 1:7

I sought the LORD, and He heard me,
And delivered me from all my fears.

PSALM 34:4

God is our refuge and strength,
A very present help in trouble.
Therefore we will not fear,
Even though the earth be removed,
And though the mountains be carried into the
    midst of the sea.

Psalm 46:1-2

The fear of man brings a snare,
but whoever trusts in the LORD shall be safe.

Proverbs 29:25

Never forget that you are where
you are today because
God has kept you and sustained you.

He shall cover you with His feathers,
And under His wings you shall take refuge;
His truth shall be your shield and buckler.
You shall not be afraid of the terror by night,
Nor of the arrow that flies by day.

Psalm 91:4-5

Don't miss out on
your tomorrow by
focusing on yesterday.

Finances

---

*A blessing is far more than money — it is
the empowerment to prosper and succeed.*

I pray that you may prosper in all things and be
in health, just as your soul prospers.

3 JOHN 2

Do not worry, saying, "What shall we eat?" or
"What shall we drink?" or "What shall we wear?"
For after all these things the Gentiles seek. For
your heavenly Father knows that you need all
these things. But seek first the kingdom of God
and His righteousness, and all these things shall
be added to you.

MATTHEW 6:31-33

I have been young, and now am old; yet I have not seen the righteous forsaken, nor his descendants begging bread.

<small>PSALM 37:25</small>

My God shall supply all your need according to His riches in glory by Christ Jesus.

<small>PHILIPPIANS 4:19</small>

Give to receive.

The LORD is my shepherd; I shall not want.

<small>PSALM 23:1</small>

The LORD will grant you plenty of goods, in the fruit of your body, in the increase of your livestock, and in the produce of your ground, in the land of which the LORD swore to your fathers to give you. The LORD will open to you His good treasure, the heavens, to give the rain to your land in its season, and to bless all the

work of your hand. You shall lend to many nations, but you shall not borrow . . . if you heed the commandments of the LORD your God, which I command you today, and are careful to observe them.

DEUTERONOMY 28:11-13

Give, and it will be given to you: good measure, pressed down, shaken together, and running over will be put into your bosom. For with the same measure that you use, it will be measured back to you.

LUKE 6:38

True riches come from God.

On the first day of the week let each one of you lay something aside, storing up as he may prosper, that there be no collections when I come.

I CORINTHIANS 16:2

But this I say: He who sows sparingly will also reap sparingly, and he who sows bountifully will also reap bountifully. So let each one give as he purposes in his heart, not grudgingly or of necessity; for God loves a cheerful giver. And God is able to make all grace abound toward you, that you, always having all sufficiency in all things, may have an abundance for every good work.

2 CORINTHIANS 9:6-8

The generous soul will be made rich,
and he who waters will also be watered himself.

PROVERBS 11:25

The young lions lack and suffer hunger; but those who seek the LORD shall not lack any good thing.

PSALM 34:10

*What leaves your hand
determines what leaves God's hand.*

Forgiveness

Forgiveness is as much a gift to yourself
as to the one who wronged you.

In Him we have redemption through His blood,
the forgiveness of sins, according to the riches of
His grace.

EPHESIANS 1:7

You have forgiven the iniquity of Your people;
You have covered all their sin.

PSALM 85:2

As far as the east is from the west,
So far has He removed our transgressions from us.

PSALM 103:12

My little children, these things I write to you,
so that you may not sin. And if anyone sins,
we have an Advocate with the Father, Jesus
Christ the righteous.

1 JOHN 2:1

*You must let go of yesterday
to take possession of tomorrow.*

If we confess our sins, He is faithful and just to forgive us our sins and to cleanse us from all unrighteousness.

1 JOHN 1:9

I will be merciful to their unrighteousness, and their sins and their lawless deeds I will remember no more.

HEBREWS 8:12

Let the wicked forsake his way,
And the unrighteous man his thoughts;
Let him return to the LORD,
And He will have mercy on him;
And to our God,
For He will abundantly pardon.

ISAIAH 55:7

We are the sum total
of the choices we make every day.

If you forgive men their trespasses, your heavenly Father will also forgive you. But if you do not forgive men their trespasses, neither will your Father forgive your trespasses.

MATTHEW 6:14-15

Then Peter came to Him and said, "Lord, how often shall my brother sin against me, and I forgive him? Up to seven times?" Jesus said to him, "I do not say to you, up to seven times, but up to seventy times seven."

MATTHEW 18:21-22

Bearing with one another, and forgiving one another, if anyone has a complaint against another; even as Christ forgave you, so you also must do.

COLOSSIANS 3:13

Grief

*When you can't trace God's hand,
trust His heart.*

The Lord has comforted His people, and will
have mercy on His afflicted.
ISAIAH 49:13B

Blessed are those who mourn, for they shall
be comforted.
MATTHEW 5:4

This is my comfort in my affliction, for Your
Word has given me life.
PSALM 119:50

O Death, where is your sting? O Hades, where
is your victory? The sting of death is sin, and
the strength of sin is the law. But thanks be to
God, who gives us the victory through our Lord
Jesus Christ.
I CORINTHIANS 15:55-57

Who can wipe a tear that will not fall?

God will wipe away every tear from their eyes;
there shall be no more death, nor sorrow, nor
crying. There shall be no more pain, for the
former things have passed away.

REVELATION 21:4

Fear not, for I am with you;
Be not dismayed, for I am your God.
I will strengthen you,
Yes, I will help you,
I will uphold you with My righteous right hand.

ISAIAH 41:10

He heals the brokenhearted and binds up
their wounds.

PSALM 147:3

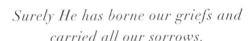

Surely He has borne our griefs and carried all our sorrows.

Cast your burden on the LORD, and He shall sustain you; He shall never permit the righteous to be moved.

Psalm 55:22

I am persuaded that neither death nor life, nor angels nor principalities nor powers, nor things present nor things to come, nor height nor depth, nor any other created thing, shall be able to separate us from the love of God which is in Christ Jesus our Lord.

Romans 8:38-39

God's time to appear for His people is when their strength is gone. And he said unto me, My grace is sufficient for thee: for my strength is made perfect in weakness.

2 Corinthians 12:9

Healing

A wound is an event—healing is a process.

Heal me, O Lord, and I shall be healed; save me, and I shall be saved, for You are my praise.

|EREMIAH 17:14

Is anyone among you sick? Let him call for the elders of the church, and let them pray over him, anointing him with oil in the name of the Lord. And the prayer of faith will save the sick, and the Lord will raise him up. And if he has committed sins, he will be forgiven.

|AMES 5:14-15

You will keep him in perfect peace,
Whose mind is stayed on You,

Because he trusts in You.
Trust in the LORD forever,
For in YAH, the LORD, is everlasting strength.

ISAIAH 26:3-4

Who Himself bore our sins in His own body on
the tree, that we, having died to sins, might live for
righteousness—by whose stripes you were healed.

I PETER 2:24

The only difference between black coal
and a precious diamond
is the amount of pressure it endured.

Those who wait on the LORD
Shall renew their strength;
They shall mount up with wings like eagles,
They shall run and not be weary,
They shall walk and not faint.

ISAIAH 40:28-29, 31

Therefore strengthen the hands which hang down, and the feeble knees, and make straight paths for your feet, so that what is lame may not be dislocated, but rather be healed. Pursue peace with all people, and holiness, without which no one will see the Lord.

HEBREWS 12:11-14

When troubles rain...let God reign.

Therefore we do not lose heart. Even though our outward man is perishing, yet the inward man is being renewed day by day. For our light affliction, which is but for a moment, is working for us a far more exceeding and eternal weight of glory, while we do not look at the things which are seen, but at the things which are not seen. For the things which are seen are temporary, but the things which are not seen are eternal.

2 CORINTHIANS 4:15-18

Health

Work hard and play hard.

"I will restore health to you and heal you of your wounds," says the LORD.
JEREMIAH 30:17

My son, give attention to my words; incline your ear to my sayings. Do not let them depart from your eyes; keep them in the midst of your heart; for they are life to those who find them, and health to all their flesh.
PROVERBS 4:20-22

Beloved, I pray that you may prosper in all things and be in health, just as your soul prospers.

3 JOHN 2

But I discipline my body and bring it into subjection, lest, when I have preached to others, I myself should become disqualified.

1 CORINTHIANS 9:27

Learn to laugh – you will live longer.

Pleasant words are like a honeycomb, sweetness to the soul and health to the bones.

PROVERBS 16:24

Do you not know that your body is the temple of the Holy Spirit who is in you, whom you have from God, and you are not your own? For you were bought at a price; therefore glorify God in your body and in your spirit, which are God's.

1 CORINTHIANS 6:19-20

And on the seventh day God ended his work which he had made; and he rested on the seventh day from all his work which he had made.

GENESIS 2:2

Life has to be managed to be effective.

I beseech you therefore, brethren, by the mercies of God, that you present your bodies a living sacrifice, holy, acceptable to God, which is your reasonable service.

ROMANS 12:1

Here is what I have seen: It is good and fitting for one to eat and drink, and to enjoy the good of all his labor in which he toils under the sun all the days of his life which God gives him; for it is his heritage.

ECCLESIASTES 5:18

Your future is found in your daily routine.
Successful people do
daily what others do occasionally.

Hearing from God

Limit your distractions
and you will hear God's voice.

When he brings out his own sheep, he goes
before them; and the sheep follow him, for they
know his voice. Yet they will by no means follow
a stranger, but will flee from him, for they do
not know the voice of strangers.

JOHN 10:4-5

He is our God, and we are the people of
His pasture, and the sheep of His hand.
Today, if you will hear His voice:
"Do not harden your hearts."

PSALM 95:7-8

Obey My voice, and I will be your God, and you shall be My people. And walk in all the ways that I have commanded you, that it may be well with you.

JEREMIAH 7:23

*God does not call us to failure,
He calls us to fulfillment.*

Now it shall come to pass, if you diligently obey the voice of the LORD your God, to observe carefully all His commandments which I command you today, that the LORD your God will set you high above all nations of the earth. And all these blessings shall come upon you and overtake you, because you obey the voice of the LORD your God.

DEUTERONOMY 28:1-2

Teach me to do Your will,
for You are my God;
Your Spirit is good.
Lead me in the land of uprightness.

I will instruct you and teach you in the way you
should go; I will guide you with My eye.

Your word is a lamp to my feet and a light to
my path.

Teach me, O LORD, the way of Your statutes,
and I shall keep it to the end.

*You must hear His voice until it becomes
louder than any other voice in your life.*

Love

You cannot love others
until you love yourself; you cannot truly
love yourself until you know
and experience God's love for you.

Beloved, let us love one another, for love is of God; and everyone who loves is born of God and knows God. He who does not love does not know God, for God is love.

1 JOHN 4:7-8

In this is love, not that we loved God, but that He loved us and sent His Son to be the propitiation for our sins. Beloved, if God so loved us, we also ought to love one another. No one has seen God at any time. If we love

one another, God abides in us, and His love has
been perfected in us.

1 JOHN 4:10-12

He who has My commandments and keeps
them, it is he who loves Me. And he who loves
Me will be loved by My Father, and I will love
him and manifest Myself to him.

JOHN 14:21

*Fulfillment is found
when you know the love of God.*

As the Father loved Me, I also have loved you;
abide in My love. If you keep My commandments,
you will abide in My love, just as I have kept My
Father's commandments and abide in His love.

JOHN 15:9-10

The LORD has appeared of old to me, saying:
"Yes, I have loved you with an everlasting love;
Therefore with lovingkindness I have drawn you."

JEREMIAH 31:3

The Father Himself loves you, because you have
loved Me, and have believed that I came forth
from God.

JOHN 16:27

---

*Never insult God's sacrifice
by questioning His love.*

God demonstrates His own love toward us,
in that while we were still sinners, Christ died
for us.

ROMANS 5:8

God so loved the world that He gave His only
begotten Son, that whoever believes in Him
should not perish but have everlasting life.

JOHN 3:16

Marriage

*When we receive God's love we are
then able to pour out His love into the
people He brings into our lives. If you are
to be the spouse God has destined
you to be, you must have love to give.*

He who finds a wife finds a good thing, and
obtains favor from the LORD.

PROVERBS 18:22

Wives, submit to your own husbands, as to the
Lord. For the husband is head of the wife, as
also Christ is head of the church; and He is the
Savior of the body. Therefore, just as the church
is subject to Christ, so let the wives be to their
own husbands in everything.

Husbands, love your wives, just as Christ also loved the church and gave Himself for her, that He might sanctify and cleanse her with the washing of water by the word, that He might present her to Himself a glorious church, not having spot or wrinkle or any such thing, but that she should be holy and without blemish. So husbands ought to love their own wives as their own bodies; he who loves his wife loves himself. For no one ever hated his own flesh, but nourishes and cherishes it, just as the Lord does the church.

EPHESIANS 5:22–31

———

*Before entering into the covenant
of marriage, find a partner who has
the desired character and qualities on the
inside, then make certain that you are
both moving toward the same goals in life.*

———

The value of a person cannot be determined by the outside packaging... the true treasure lies within.

Love does no harm to a neighbor; therefore love is the fulfillment of the law.

ROMANS 13:10

Houses and riches are an inheritance from fathers, but a prudent wife is from the Lord.

PROVERBS 19:14

Who can find a virtuous wife?
For her worth is far above rubies.
The heart of her husband safely trusts her;
so he will have no lack of gain.
She does him good and not evil
all the days of her life.
Her children rise up and call her blessed;
her husband also, and he praises her.

PROVERBS 31:10–12, 28

Mentors

Your mentor is your coach,
not your friend.

That which we have seen and heard we declare
to you, that you also may have fellowship with
us; and truly our fellowship is with the Father
and with His Son Jesus Christ. But if we walk
in the light as He is in the light, we have
fellowship with one another, and the blood of
Jesus Christ His Son cleanses us from all sin.

1 JOHN 1:3, 7

Let the word of Christ dwell in you richly in all
wisdom, teaching and admonishing one another
in psalms and hymns and spiritual songs,
singing with grace in your hearts to the Lord.

COLOSSIANS 3:16

That their hearts may be encouraged, being knit together in love, and attaining to all riches of the full assurance of understanding, to the knowledge of the mystery of God, both of the Father and of Christ.

COLOSSIANS 2:2

Mentors are your gate to greatness and your bridge to blessings.

We took sweet counsel together, and walked to the house of God in the throng.

PSALM 55:14

Let your light so shine before men, that they may see your good works and glorify your Father in heaven.

MATTHEW 5:16

Therefore, as we have opportunity, let us do good to all, especially to those who are of the household of faith.

GALATIANS 6:10

If you instruct the brethren in these things, you will be a good minister of Jesus Christ, nourished in the words of faith and of the good doctrine which you have carefully followed.

1 TIMOTHY 4:6

Having then gifts differing according to the grace that is given to us, let us use them: if prophecy, let us prophesy in proportion to our faith; or ministry, let us use it in our ministering; he who teaches, in teaching; he who exhorts, in exhortation.

ROMANS 12:5

A person can lead you only as far as that person can "see" with his faith.

Obedience

You are the captain of your own vessel —
you choose the direction of your life.

Blessed *are* those who hear the word of God and
keep it!"

LUKE 11:28

Behold, I set before you today a blessing and a
curse: the blessing, if you obey the
commandments of the LORD your God which I
command you today; and the curse, if you do
not obey the commandments of the LORD your
God, but turn aside from the way which I
command you today, to go after other gods
which you have not known.

DEUTERONOMY 11:26–28

To obey is better than sacrifice, and to heed
than the fat of rams.

1 Samuel 15:22

Disobedience to God's Word
delays your destiny.

Oh, that you had heeded My commandments!
Then your peace would have been like a river,
and your righteousness like the waves of the sea.

Isaiah 48:18

Obey My voice, and I will be your God, and you
shall be My people. And walk in all the ways that I
have commanded you, that it may be well with you.

Jeremiah 7:23

If you love Me, keep My commandments. He
who has My commandments and keeps them, it
is he who loves Me. And he who loves Me will

be loved by My Father, and I will love him and
manifest Myself to him.

J OHN 14:15, 21

Though He was a Son, yet He learned obedience
by the things which He suffered.

HEBREWS 5:8

The commandments of God are
entrance into the Kingdom of God.

Now by this we know that we know Him,
if we keep His commandments. He who says,
"I know Him," and does not keep His
commandments, is a liar, and the truth is not in
him. But whoever keeps His word, truly the
love of God is perfected in him. By this we
know that we are in Him. He who says he
abides in Him ought himself also to walk just as
He walked.

1 J OHN 2:3–6

The people said to Joshua, "The Lord our God
we will serve, and His voice we will obey!"

JOSHUA 24:24

I have hoped in Your ordinances.
So shall I keep Your law continually,
forever and ever.

PSALM 119:42

We ought to obey God rather than men.

ACTS 5:29

So if you walk in My ways, to keep My statutes
and My commandments, as your father David
walked, then I will lengthen your days.

1 KINGS 3:14

Obey those who rule over you, and be submissive,
for they watch out for your souls, as those who
must give account. Let them do so with joy and not
with grief, for that would be unprofitable for you.

HEBREWS 13:17

Peace

*God's peace comforts you
from the harsh realities of life.*

You will keep him in perfect peace, whose mind
is stayed on You, because he trusts in You.

ISAIAH 26:3

He Himself is our peace, who has made both
one, and has broken down the middle wall
of separation.

EPHESIANS 2:13, 14

The God of peace will crush Satan under your
feet shortly. The grace of our Lord Jesus Christ
be with you. Amen.

ROMANS 16:20

The things which you learned and received and
heard and saw in me, these do, and the God of
peace will be with you.

PHILIPPIANS 4:9

Peace is the proof of God's presence.

Let the peace of God rule in your hearts, to which also you were called in one body; and be thankful.

COLOSSIANS 3:15

The LORD will give strength to His people; the LORD will bless His people with peace.

PSALM 29:11

Peace I leave with you, My peace I give to you; not as the world gives do I give to you. Let not your heart be troubled, neither let it be afraid.

JOHN 14:27

LORD, You will establish peace for us, for You have also done all our works in us.

ISAIAH 26:12

Know God... Know Peace

You shall go out with joy,
And be led out with peace;
The mountains and the hills
Shall break forth into singing before you,
And all the trees of the field shall clap their hands.

ISAIAH 55:12

Mark the blameless man, and observe the
upright; for the future of that man is peace.

PSALM 37:37

To be carnally minded is death, but to be
spiritually minded is life and peace.

ROMANS 8:6

He shall enter into peace; they shall rest in their
beds, each one walking in his uprightness.

ISAIAH 57:2

The kingdom of God is not eating and drinking, but righteousness and peace and joy in the Holy Spirit. For he who serves Christ in these things is acceptable to God and approved by men. Therefore let us pursue the things which make for peace and the things by which one may edify another.

ROMANS 14:17–19

Great peace have those who love Your law, and nothing causes them to stumble.

PSALM 119:165

The meek shall inherit the earth, and shall delight themselves in the abundance of peace.

PSALM 37:11

May the God of hope fill you with all joy and peace in believing, that you may abound in hope by the power of the Holy Spirit.

ROMANS 15:13

Be flexible. You will need to bend in life.

Perseverance

You are built for it! It is God's strength poured into us and working through us that enables us to overcome, to persevere, and to be strong.

Since we are surrounded by so great a cloud of witnesses, let us lay aside every weight, and the sin which so easily ensnares us, and let us run with endurance the race that is set before us.

HEBREWS 12:1

Whatever is born of God overcomes the world. And this is the victory that has overcome the world—our faith.

1 JOHN 5:4

I know whom I have believed and am persuaded

that He is able to keep what I have committed
to Him until that Day.

2 TIMOTHY 1:12

Do not become sluggish, but imitate those who
through faith and patience inherit the promises.

HEBREWS 6:12

———————

Just keep walking…
He will see you through!

———————

Knowing that the testing of your faith produces
patience. But let patience have its perfect work, that
you may be perfect and complete, lacking nothing.

JAMES 1:3, 4

It is good that one should hope and wait quietly
for the salvation of the LORD.

LAMENTATIONS 3:26

If we hope for what we do not see, we eagerly
wait for it with perseverance.

ROMANS 8:25

*You are where you are today because God
has kept you and sustained you.*

In all these things we are more than conquerors
through Him who loved us.
ROMANS 8:37

Giving all diligence, add to your faith virtue, to
virtue knowledge, to knowledge self-control, to
self-control perseverance, to perseverance
godliness, to godliness brotherly kindness, and
to brotherly kindness love. For if these things
are yours and abound, you will be neither
barren nor unfruitful in the knowledge of our
Lord Jesus Christ.
2 PETER 1:5–8

Praise/Worship

Praise is thanking God for what He has done.
Worship recognizes God for who He is.

You are a chosen generation, a royal priesthood,
a holy nation, His own special people, that you
may proclaim the praises of Him who called
you out of darkness into His marvelous light.

1 PETER 2:9

Therefore by Him let us continually offer the
sacrifice of praise to God, that is, the fruit of
our lips, giving thanks to His name.

HEBREWS 13:15

Praise the LORD!
For it is good to sing praises to our God;
For it is pleasant, and praise is beautiful.

PSALM 147:1

*When you praise you take your focus
off the adversity and place it on the blessing
that God has ahead for you.*

I will call upon the LORD, who is worthy to be
praised; so shall I be saved from my enemies.

2 SAMUEL 22:4

I will bless the LORD at all times; His praise
shall continually be in my mouth.

PSALM 34:1

Sing praises to God, sing praises!
Sing praises to our King, sing praises!
For God is the King of all the earth;
Sing praises with understanding.

PSALM 47:6–7

Great is the LORD, and greatly to be praised in
the city of our God, in His holy mountain.

PSALM 48:1

*The more you praise God for who He is,
the more you experience His infinite and
unchanging care, provision, and protection.*

Whoever offers praise glorifies Me; and to him
who orders his conduct aright I will show the
salvation of God.

PSALM 50:23

Because Your lovingkindness is better than life,
My lips shall praise You.
Thus I will bless You while I live;
I will lift up my hands in Your name.
My soul shall be satisfied as with marrow
    and fatness,
And my mouth shall praise You with joyful lips.

PSALM 63:3–5

It is good to give thanks to the LORD, and to
sing praises to Your name, O Most High.

PSALM 92:1

Let my mouth be filled with Your praise
And with Your glory all the day.
But I will hope continually,
And will praise You yet more and more.

PSALM 71:8, 14

The LORD is great and greatly to be praised;
He is to be feared above all gods.

PSALM 96:4

Challenge yourself to give God
an advance praise before you receive
your breakthrough.

Oh, that men would give thanks to the LORD
for His goodness, and for His wonderful works
to the children of men!

PSALM 107:8

Prayer

Pray now or Pay later!

It shall come to pass that before they call, I will answer; and while they are still speaking, I will hear.

ISAIAH 65:24

Ask, and it will be given to you; seek, and you will find; knock, and it will be opened to you. For everyone who asks receives, and he who seeks finds, and to him who knocks it will be opened.

MATTHEW 7:7–8

Whatever things you ask in prayer, believing, you will receive.

MATTHEW 21:22

And whatever you ask in My name, that I will do, that the Father may be glorified in the Son.

JOHN 14:13

Much Prayer...Much Power,
Little Prayer...Little Power,
No Prayer...No Power.

I say to you that if two of you agree on earth concerning anything that they ask, it will be done for them by My Father in heaven. For where two or three are gathered together in My name, I am there in the midst of them.

MATTHEW 18:19–20

If you abide in Me, and My words abide in you, you will ask what you desire, and it shall be done for you.

JOHN 15:7

Delight yourself also in the LORD, and He shall give you the desires of your heart.

PSALM 37:4

Let us therefore come boldly to the throne of grace, that we may obtain mercy and find grace to help in time of need.

HEBREWS 4:16

We govern the nations on our knees.

In that day you will ask Me nothing. Most assuredly, I say to you, whatever you ask the Father in My name He will give you.

JOHN 16:23

He shall call upon Me, and I will answer him; I will be with him in trouble; I will deliver him and honor him.

PSALM 91:15

The LORD is near to all who call upon Him, to all who call upon Him in truth.
He will fulfill the desire of those who fear Him;
He also will hear their cry and save them.

PSALM 145:18–19

The Lord is far from the wicked, but He hears the prayer of the righteous.

PROVERBS 15:29

Prayer places you in the King's chamber.

Call to Me, and I will answer you, and show you great and mighty things, which you do not know.

JEREMIAH 33:3

But you, when you pray, go into your room, and when you have shut your door, pray to your Father who is in the secret place; and your Father who sees in secret will reward you openly.

MATTHEW 6:6

Whatever we ask we receive from Him, because we keep His commandments and do those things that are pleasing in His sight.

1 JOHN 3:22

Prosperity

Speak the Word, meditate on the Word,
and act on the Word—
then *will you have prosperity and success.*

This Book of the Law shall not depart from your
mouth, but you shall meditate in it day and
night, that you may observe to do according to
all that is written in it. For then you will make
your way prosperous, and then you will have
good success.

JOSHUA 1:8

Wisdom brings success.

ECCLESIASTES 10:10

And you shall remember the LORD your God,
for it is He who gives you power to get wealth.

DEUTERONOMY 8:18

Success has a price — prosperity has value.

Let them shout for joy and be glad, who favor my righteous cause; and let them say continually, "Let the LORD be magnified, who has pleasure in the prosperity of His servant.?"

PSALM 35:27

Beloved, I pray that you may prosper in all things and be in health, just as your soul prospers.

3 JOHN 2

The LORD will command the blessing on you in your storehouses and in all to which you set your hand, and He will bless you in the land which the LORD your God is giving you. The LORD will establish you as a holy people to Himself, just as He has sworn to you, if you keep the commandments of the LORD your God and walk in His ways.

DEUTERONOMY 28:8–9

*If it's too much to give...
it's too much to receive.*

"Bring all the tithes into the storehouse,
that there may be food in My house,
and try Me now in this," says the LORD of hosts,
"If I will not open for you the windows of heaven
and pour out for you such blessing that there will
not be room enough to receive it."

MALACHI 3:10

Then you will prosper, if you take care to fulfill
the statutes and judgments with which the LORD
charged Moses concerning Israel. Be strong and
of good courage; do not fear nor be dismayed.

I CHRONICLES 22:13

❋

God will bring you out of
the land of not enough
(Egypt) and through
the land of just enough
(wilderness) into
the land of more than
enough (Canaan).

Provision

God honors His Word above
His name…what He said He will do,
that He shall surely do.

Thus says the LORD, your Redeemer,
The Holy One of Israel:
"I am the LORD your God,
Who teaches you to profit,
Who leads you by the way you should go."

ISAIAH 48:17

The young lions lack and suffer hunger;
but those who seek the LORD shall not lack any
good thing.

PSALM 34:10

Through wisdom a house is built,
and by understanding it is established;
by knowledge the rooms are filled
with all precious and pleasant riches.

PROVERBS 24:3–4

---

*God's Word brings wholeness
to whom it is sent.*

Be anxious for nothing, but in everything by
prayer and supplication, with thanksgiving,
let your requests be made known to God;
and the peace of God, which surpasses all
understanding, will guard your hearts and minds
through Christ Jesus.

PHILIPPIANS 4:6–7

Who provides food for the raven, when its
young ones cry to God, and wander about for
lack of food?

JOB 38:41

Are not two sparrows sold for a copper coin? And not one of them falls to the ground apart from your Father's will. But the very hairs of your head are all numbered. Do not fear therefore; you are of more value than many sparrows.

MATTHEW 10:29–31

You can do what God says you can do, you can have what God says you can have. Our God is limitless!

The horse is prepared for the day of battle, But deliverance is of the LORD.

PROVERBS 21:31

If you then, being evil, know how to give good gifts to your children, how much more will your Father who is in heaven give good things to those who ask Him!

MATTHEW 7:11

God is in you to produce excellence.

Relationships

Love covers many sins.

Do not be deceived: "Evil company corrupts good habits."

I CORINTHIANS 15:33

Live joyfully with the wife whom you love all the days of your vain life which He has given you under the sun, all your days of vanity; for that is your portion in life, and in the labor which you perform under the sun.

ECCLESIASTES 9:9

Let this mind be in you which was also in Christ Jesus, who, being in the form of God, did not consider it robbery to be equal with God, but made Himself of no reputation,

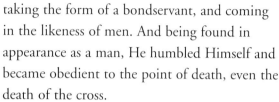

taking the form of a bondservant, and coming in the likeness of men. And being found in appearance as a man, He humbled Himself and became obedient to the point of death, even the death of the cross.

PHILIPPIANS 2:5–8

*Find your place in the love of God,
and you'll find your place in the hearts
of those God puts in your life.*

I am a companion of all who fear You, and of those who keep Your precepts.

PSALM 119:63

By this we know love, because He laid down His life for us. And we also ought to lay down our lives for the brethren.

1 JOHN 3:16

Above all these things put on love, which is the bond of perfection.

COLOSSIANS 3:14

Finally, all of you be of one mind, having compassion for one another; love as brothers, be tenderhearted, be courteous; not returning evil for evil or reviling for reviling, but on the contrary blessing, knowing that you were called to this, that you may inherit a blessing.

1 PETER 3:8–9

_True friends are like diamonds,
precious and rare._

Faithful are the wounds of a friend,
But the kisses of an enemy are deceitful.

PROVERBS 27:6

As iron sharpens iron,
So a man sharpens the countenance of his friend.

PROVERBS 27:17

Bear one another's burdens, and so fulfill the law of Christ.

GALATIANS 6:2

That their hearts may be encouraged, being knit together in love, and attaining to all riches of the full assurance of understanding, to the knowledge of the mystery of God, both of the Father and of Christ.

COLOSSIANS 2:2

We cannot fully know who we are,
until we know who God is.

Now may the God of patience and comfort grant you to be like-minded toward one another, according to Christ Jesus, that you may with one mind and one mouth glorify the God and Father of our Lord Jesus Christ. Therefore receive one another, just as Christ also received us, to the glory of God.

ROMANS 15:5–7

Restoration

---

*God will wash you with His mercy
to reveal the brilliance in you.*

I rejoice, not that you were made sorry, but that
your sorrow led to repentance. For you were
made sorry in a godly manner, that you might
suffer loss from us in nothing. For godly sorrow
produces repentance leading to salvation, not to
be regretted; but the sorrow of the world
produces death.

2 CORINTHIANS 7:9–10

The LORD raises those who are bowed down;
the LORD loves the righteous.

PSALM 146:8

They shall rebuild the old ruins,
They shall raise up the former desolations,

And they shall repair the ruined cities,
The desolations of many generations. . . .
They shall call you the servants of our God.

ISAIAH 61:4–6

Depleted people can become hurting
and desperate people.
But . . . God offers us restoration.

Behold, I will do a new thing,
Now it shall spring forth;
Shall you not know it
I will even make a road in the wilderness
And rivers in the desert.

ISAIAH 43:19

I will restore to you the years that the swarming
locust has eaten. . . .You shall eat in plenty and
be satisfied, and praise the name of the Lord
your God, who has dealt wondrously with you;
and My people shall never be put to shame.

JOEL 2:25–26

He gives power to the weak,
And to those who have no might He increases
strength.

ISAIAH 40:29

As for you, you meant evil against me; but God
meant it for good.

GENESIS 50:20

He restores my soul;
He leads me in the paths of righteousness
for His name's sake.

PSALM 23:3

---

*God can change your life
with just one touch of His hand.*

I will heal their backsliding,
I will love them freely,
for My anger has turned away from him.

HOSEA 14:4

When God restores you,
He brings you to wholeness.

"I will seek what was lost and bring back what
was driven away, bind up the broken and
strengthen what was sick."

 EZEKIEL 34:16

He who covers his sins will not prosper,
but whoever confesses and forsakes them will
have mercy.

PROVERBS 28:13

Love doesn't dismiss sin as sin—
no, it "covers" sin with understanding,
with compassion, with a
humble admission that "there but for
the grace of God, go I."

Self-Control

To walk in the Spirit is to be
synchronized with God.

No one can serve two masters; for either he will
hate the one and love the other, or else he will
be loyal to the one and despise the other. You
cannot serve God and mammon.

MATTHEW 6:24

Forsake foolishness and live, and go in the way
of understanding. "The fear of the LORD is the
beginning of wisdom, and the knowledge of the
Holy One is understanding."

PROVERBS 9:6, 10

The fear of the LORD leads to life, and he who has it will abide in satisfaction; he will not be visited with evil.

PROVERBS 19:23

Let your light so shine before men, that they may see your good works and glorify your Father in heaven.

MATTHEW 5:16

*You can't plead promises
and violate principles.*

Let your heart therefore be loyal to the Lord our God, to walk in His statutes and keep His commandments, as at this day.

I KINGS 8:60–61

Be doers of the word, and not hearers only, deceiving yourselves.

JAMES 1:22

Now therefore, if you will indeed obey My voice
and keep My covenant, then you shall be a
special treasure to Me above all people; for all
the earth is Mine.

EXODUS 19:5

Do not be deceived, God is not mocked; for
whatever a man sows, that he will also reap. For
he who sows to his flesh will of the flesh reap
corruption, but he who sows to the Spirit will of
the Spirit reap everlasting life.

GALATIANS 6:7–8

If you love Me, keep My commandments.

JOHN 14:15

You don't violate what you value.

But Peter and the other apostles answered and
said: "We ought to obey God rather than men."

ACTS 5:29

Paula White ☙ 151

I discipline my body and bring it into subjection, lest, when I have preached to others, I myself should become disqualified.

1 CORINTHIANS 9:27

Casting down arguments and every high thing that exalts itself against the knowledge of God, bringing every thought into captivity to the obedience of Christ.

2 CORINTHIANS 10:5

Whoever has no rule over his own spirit is like a city broken down, without walls.

PROVERBS 25:28

The God who has prepared
a blessing for you is the God who is
preparing you for the blessing.

Self-Esteem

*You are more than
what you see in the mirror.*

For we are His workmanship, created in Christ
Jesus for good works, which God prepared
beforehand that we should walk in them.

EPHESIANS 2:10

For You formed my inward parts;
You covered me in my mother's womb.
I will praise You, for I am fearfully and
    wonderfully made;
Marvelous are Your works,
And that my soul knows very well.

PSALM 139:13–14

He has made everything beautiful in its time.

ECCLESIASTES 3:11

You are a chosen generation, a royal priesthood, a holy nation, His own special people, that you may proclaim the praises of Him who called you out of darkness into His marvelous light.

I PETER 2:9

You are a Designer's Original...
created for a purpose.

God created man in His own image; in the image of God He created him; male and female He created them.

GENESIS 1:27

Before I formed you in the womb I knew you; before you were born I sanctified you.

JEREMIAH 1:5

Being confident of this very thing, that He who has begun a good work in you will complete it until the day of Jesus Christ.

PHILIPPIANS 1:6

The LORD takes pleasure in His people;
He will beautify the humble with salvation.

PSALM 149:4

Your hands have made me and fashioned me;
give me understanding, that I may learn
    Your commandments.
Those who fear You will be glad when they see me,
Because I have hoped in Your word.

PSALM 119:73–73

If anyone is in Christ, he is a new creation;
old things have passed away; behold, all things
have become new.

2 CORINTHIANS 5:17

---

*God designed you perfectly
for the assignment on your life.*

*Your true self is made up
of your deepest desires,
gifts, abilities,
dreams, and passions.
Your true self is
what God created in you.*

Stress Management

If you fail to plan, you plan to fail.

Commit your way to the LORD,
Trust also in Him,
And He shall bring it to pass.
He shall bring forth your righteousness as the light,
And your justice as the noonday.
Rest in the LORD, and wait patiently for Him.

PSALM 37:5–7

There remains therefore a rest for the people of God. Let us therefore be diligent to enter that rest, lest anyone fall according to the same example of disobedience. Seeing then that we have a great High Priest who has passed through the heavens, Jesus the Son of God, let us hold fast our confession.

HEBREWS 4:9, 11, 14

He said, "My Presence will go with you, and I will give you rest."

EXODUS 33:14

Those who sow in tears shall reap in joy.

PSALM 126:6

Guard your thoughts.

Do not worry about your life, what you will eat; nor about the body, what you will put on. Life is more than food, and the body is more than clothing. Consider the ravens, for they neither sow nor reap, which have neither storehouse nor barn; and God feeds them. Of how much more value are you than the birds? And which of you by worrying can add one cubit to his stature? If you then are not able to do the least, why are you anxious for the rest?

God is not the author of confusion but of peace, as in all the churches of the saints.

I CORINTHIANS 14:33

Cast your burden on the LORD, and He shall sustain you; He shall never permit the righteous to be moved.

PSALM 55:22

You cannot conquer what you won't confront, you cannot confront what you won't identify.

Consider the lilies, how they grow: they neither toil nor spin; and yet I say to you, even Solomon in all his glory was not arrayed like one of these. If then God so clothes the grass, which today is in the field and tomorrow is thrown into the oven, how much more will He clothe you, O you of little faith?

LUKE 12:22–28

Trust in the LORD with all your heart, and lean not on your own understanding; in all your

ways acknowledge Him, and He shall direct
your paths.

PROVERBS 3:5–6

Search me, O God, and know my heart;
Try me, and know my anxieties;
And see if *there is any* wicked way in me,
And lead me in the way everlasting.

PSALM 139:23–24

_____

If God called you...He will equip you.

_____

Better is a dry morsel with quietness,
than a house full of feasting with strife.

PROVERBS 17:1

A man's heart plans his way,
but the LORD directs his steps.

PROVERBS 16:9

Talents

Maximize your potential.

A man's gift makes room for him,
And brings him before great men.

PROVERBS 18:16

If anyone speaks, let him speak as the oracles of
God. If anyone ministers, let him do it as with
the ability which God supplies, that in all things
God may be glorified through Jesus Christ, to
whom belong the glory and the dominion
forever and ever.

I PETER 4:11

Delight yourself also in the LORD,
and He shall give you the desires of your heart.

PSALM 37:4

Commit your works to the LORD, and your
thoughts will be established.

PROVERBS 16:3

We have received, not the spirit of the world,
but the Spirit who is from God, that we might
know the things that have been freely given to
us by God.

1 CORINTHIANS 2:12

We serve an equal opportunity God.

There are diversities of gifts, but the same Spirit.
There are differences of ministries, but the same
Lord. And there are diversities of activities, but
it is the same God who works all in all.

1 CORINTHIANS 12:4–6

Pursue your God-given passion.

All the members do not have the same function, so we, being many, are one body in Christ, and individually members of one another. Having then gifts differing according to the grace that is given to us, let us use them: if prophecy, let us prophesy in proportion to our faith; or ministry, let us use it in our ministering; he who teaches, in teaching; he who exhorts, in exhortation; he who gives, with liberality; he who leads, with diligence; he who shows mercy, with cheerfulness.

ROMANS 12:4–8

To whom much is given, from him much will be required.

LUKE 12:48

We are not called to fulfill other people's dreams. WE are called to fulfill the dreams God has planted in us.

Thoughts

❀

You must "think big"
to do God-sized things.

To be carnally minded is death, but to be
spiritually minded is life and peace. Because the
carnal mind is enmity against God; for it is not
subject to the law of God, nor indeed can be.
So then, those who are in the flesh cannot
please God.

ROMANS 8:6–8

Let this mind be in you which was also in
Christ Jesus.

PHILIPPIANS 2:5

Set your mind on things above, not on things
on the earth.

COLOSSIANS 3:2

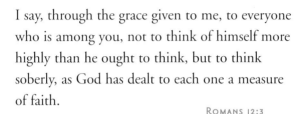

I say, through the grace given to me, to everyone who is among you, not to think of himself more highly than he ought to think, but to think soberly, as God has dealt to each one a measure of faith.

ROMANS 12:3

Our lives move in the
direction of our most dominant thoughts.

Do not be conformed to this world, but be transformed by the renewing of your mind, that you may prove what is that good and acceptable and perfect will of God.

ROMANS 12:2

Commit your works to the LORD,
and your thoughts will be established.

PROVERBS 16:3

As he thinks in his heart, so *is* he.

PROVERBS 23:7

Casting down arguments and every high thing that exalts itself against the knowledge of God, bringing every thought into captivity to the obedience of Christ.

2 Corinthians 10:5

The strength for what we do flows out of what we think or believe we are capable of doing.

Whatever things are true, whatever things are noble, whatever things are just, whatever things are pure, whatever things are lovely, whatever things are of good report, if there is any virtue and if there is anything praiseworthy—meditate on these things.

Philippians 4:8

God has not given us a spirit of fear, but of power and of love and of a sound mind.

2 Timothy 1:7

Unity

Unity is power.

Can two walk together, unless they are agreed?

"I pray for them. I do not pray for the world but for those whom You have given Me, for they are Yours. And all Mine are Yours, and Yours are Mine, and I am glorified in them. Now I am no longer in the world, but these are in the world, and I come to You. Holy Father, keep through Your name those whom You have given Me, that they may be one as We are."

JOHN 17:9–11

Do not speak evil of one another, brethren. He who speaks evil of a brother and judges his

brother, speaks evil of the law and judges the law. But if you judge the law, you are not a doer of the law but a judge. There is one Lawgiver, who is able to save and to destroy. Who are you to judge another?

JAMES 4:11–12

The wise woman builds her house, but the foolish pulls it down with her hands.

PROVERBS 14:1

God is love, and if we are filled with God's Spirit, then we can't help but love.

A new commandment I give to you, that you love one another; as I have loved you, that you also love one another.

JOHN 13:34

Now may the God of patience and comfort grant you to be like-minded toward one

another, according to Christ Jesus, that you may
with one mind and one mouth glorify the God
and Father of our Lord Jesus Christ. Therefore
receive one another, just as Christ also received
us, to the glory of God.

ROMANS 15:5–7

Let the word of Christ dwell in you richly in all
wisdom, teaching and admonishing one another
in psalms and hymns and spiritual songs,
singing with grace in your hearts to the Lord.

COLOSSIANS 3:16

Whoever desires to become great among you
shall be your servant. And whoever of you
desires to be first shall be slave of all. For even
the Son of Man did not come to be served, but
to serve, and to give His life a ransom for many.

MARK 10:43–45

A house divided cannot stand.

Now I plead with you, brethren, by the name of our Lord Jesus Christ, that you all speak the same thing, and that there be no divisions among you, but that you be perfectly joined together in the same mind and in the same judgment.

1 CORINTHIANS 1:10

Therefore, as we have opportunity, let us do good to all, especially to those who are of the household of faith.

GALATIANS 6:10

But now God has set the members, each one of them, in the body just as He pleased. And if they were all one member, where would the body be? But now indeed there are many members, yet one body. And the eye cannot say to the hand, "I have no need of you"; nor again the head to the feet, "I have no need of you." No, much rather, those members of the body which seem to be weaker are necessary.

But you, beloved, building yourselves up
on your most holy faith, praying in the Holy
Spirit, keep yourselves in the love of God,
looking for the mercy of our Lord Jesus Christ
unto eternal life.

JUDE 21

For every ailment God has a prescription.

And those members of the body which we think
to be less honorable, on these we bestow greater
honor; and our unpresentable parts have greater
modesty, but our presentable parts have no need.
But God composed the body, having given greater
honor to that part which lacks it, that there should
be no schism in the body, but that the members
should have the same care for one another.

And if one member suffers, all the members
suffer with it; or if one member is honored,

all the members rejoice with it. Now you are the body of Christ, and members individually.

1 Corinthians 12:18–27

"Where two or three are gathered together in My name, I am there in the midst of them."

Then Peter came to Him and said, "Lord, how often shall my brother sin against me, and I forgive him? Up to seven times?" Jesus said to him, "I do not say to you, up to seven times, but up to seventy times seven.

Matthew 18:20–22

*Life is too short
to think small.*

Words

Your words create your world.

Death and life are in the power of the tongue, and those who love it will eat its fruit.

PROVERBS 18:21

He who guards his mouth preserves his life, but he who opens wide his lips shall have destruction.

PROVERBS 13:3

But I say to you that for every idle word men may speak, they will give account of it in the day of judgment.

MATTHEW 12:36

Sing to Him, sing psalms to Him; talk of all His wondrous works!

1 CHRONICLES 16:9

What lives in your mouth
will eventually live in your life.

Do not be a witness against your neighbor
    without cause,
for would you deceive with your lips?

PROVERBS 24:28

Avoid foolish disputes, genealogies, contentions,
and strivings about the law; for they are
unprofitable and useless.

TITUS 3:9

A man has joy by the answer of his mouth,
and a word spoken in due season, how good it is!

PROVERBS 15:23

O Timothy! Guard what was committed to your
trust, avoiding the profane and idle babblings
and contradictions of what is falsely called
knowledge—by professing it some have strayed
concerning the faith. Grace be with you. Amen.

1 TIMOTHY 6:20–21

Let your WORDS *agree with God's* WORKS.

As long as my breath is in me,
and the breath of God in my nostrils,
my lips will not speak wickedness,
nor my tongue utter deceit.

|OB 27:3–4

As He who called you is holy, you also be holy
in all your conduct.

I PETER 1:15

Who, when He was reviled, did not revile in
return; when He suffered, He did not threaten,
but committed Himself to Him who
judges righteously.

I PETER 2:23

He who would love life and see good days, let
him refrain his tongue from evil, and his lips
from speaking deceit.

I PETER 3:10

If you want to know how you think,
listen to what you say.

Keep your tongue from evil,
and your lips from speaking deceit.

PSALM 34:13

The heart of the wise teaches his mouth,
and adds learning to his lips.

PROVERBS 16:23

The Lord GOD has given Me
the tongue of the learned,
that I should know how to speak
a word in season to him who is weary.

ISAIAH 50:4

God's Plan of Salvation

For all have sinned and fall short of the glory of God.

ROMANS 3:23

But God demonstrates His own love toward us, in that while we were still sinners, Christ died for us.

ROMANS 5:8

Therefore, just as through one man sin entered the world, and death through sin, and thus death spread to all men, because all sinned.

ROMANS 5:12

For the wages of sin is death, but the gift of God is eternal life in Christ Jesus our Lord.

ROMANS 6:23

For God did not send His Son into the world to condemn the world, but that the world through Him might be saved.

JOHN 3:17

He who believes in the Son has everlasting life; and he who does not believe the Son shall not see life, but the wrath of God abides on him.

JOHN 3:36

Moreover, brethren, I declare to you the gospel which I preached to you, which also you received and in which you stand, by which also you are saved, if you hold fast that word which I preached to you—unless you believed in vain. For I delivered to you first of all that which I also received: that Christ died for our sins according to the Scriptures, and that He was buried, and that He rose again the third day according to the Scriptures.

I CORINTHIANS 15:1–4

But as many as received Him, to them He gave the right to become children of God, to those who believe in His name.

JOHN 1:12

For God so loved the world that He gave His only begotten Son, that whoever believes in Him should not perish but have everlasting life.

JOHN 3:16

For by grace you have been saved through faith, and that not of yourselves; it is the gift of God, not of works, lest anyone should boast.

EPHESIANS 2:8–9

Behold, I stand at the door and knock. If anyone hears My voice and opens the door, I will come in to him and dine with him, and he with Me.

REVELATION 3:20

But what does it say? "The word is near you, in your mouth and in your heart" (that is, the word of faith which we preach): that if you confess with your mouth the Lord Jesus and believe in your heart that God has raised Him from the dead, you will be saved.

For with the heart one believes unto righteousness, and with the mouth confession is made unto salvation.

ROMANS 10:8–10

Therefore whoever confesses Me before men, him I will also confess before My Father who is in heaven.

MATTHEW 10:32

Promises for my life:

_____

_____

_____

_____

_____

_____

_____

_____

_____

_____

_____

_____

_____

Promises for my life:

_____

_____

_____

_____

_____

_____

_____

_____

_____

_____

_____

_____

_____

_____

Promises for my life:

_____

_____

_____

_____

_____

_____

_____

_____

_____

_____

_____

_____

_____

Promises for my life:

_____

_____

_____

_____

_____

_____

_____

_____

_____

_____

_____

_____

Promises for my life:

_____

_____

_____

_____

_____

_____

_____

_____

_____

_____

_____

_____

_____

Promises for my life:

_____

_____

_____

_____

_____

_____

_____

_____

_____

_____

_____

_____

_____

Resources

BOOKS BY PAULA WHITE
- *Deal With It*
- *He Loves Me, He Loves Me Not*

DEVOTIONAL GUIDES
- *Daily Treasures*
- *Morning by Morning*

LANDMARK SERMONS
(available in CD or VHS formats)
- *Can You Dig It?*
- *Have You Seen My Resume?*
- *Don't Lose the Evidence*
- *Your Friend Judas*
- *Covenant Connection*
- *The Best of the Potters House*

All products can be ordered through our eStore or
via our toll-free telephone product line.

www.paulawhite.org

1-800-992-8892

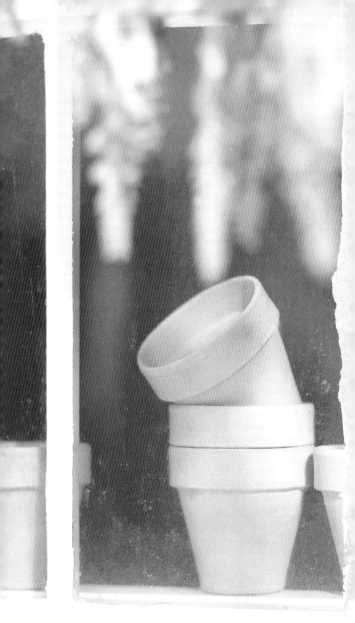

*God never leaves
your destiny in
anyone else's hand.*